KOKUMỌ

REACQUAINTED WITH LIFE

TOPSIDE
HELIOTROPE

Publisher's Note: This poetry collection is a work of fiction. Names, characters, places, and incidents either are the product of the author's imagination or are used ficticiously. Any resemblance to actual events, locales, or persons—living, dead, is totally coincidental.

Library of Congress Cataloging-in-Publication Data is available.

ISBN -- 978-1-62729-016-6

10 9 8 7 6 5 4 3 2 1

Ta
Harriet, Nina, Sylvester, Madame Sata

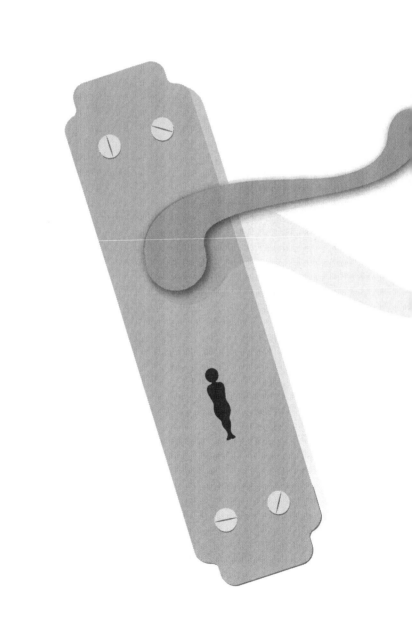

CONTENTS

PROLOGUE: GALACTIC BITCH-SLAP

1.   Rape is theft.

2.   Privilege, is amoebic.

3.   Ignorance is not a theory.

4.   Freedom, is not a competition.

5.   Home is the place where only love is allowed.

6.   You can be a murderer, and never once take a life.

7.   You, are your karma!

8.   Evry'body wanna piece ah da pie. But nobody wanna make it.

9.   The truth is never an insult.

10. Accountability is a dual process.

11. People who don't cry with their eyes, cry with their fists.

12. Sex is sacred. Religion, is vulgar.

13. Community is not currency.

14. **Pain is not a rites of passage.**

15. There are certain people you love, only when you hate yourself.

16. The presence of pleasure, does not mean the absence of rape.

17. All tears are not made equal.

18. The beautiful thing about the truth? Is that it needs no one to agree with it.

19. Tha scraps from massa table will neva equal a feast!

20. How you get it? Is just as important as if.

21. You deserve every lie you're dumb enough to believe.

22. My body, is not your trauma!

23. It'll always be easier to call me crazy, than it is to call yourself oppressive.

24. God is not a being. God, is an element.

25. Feminism, is patriarchy for people with pussies. Womanism too bitch!

26. Don't tell me what I need unless you're willing to provide it.

27. You'll never meet someone you haven't met before.

28. Never, let the ego ruin what the soul has ordained.

29. The truth cannot be told. It can only be discovered.

30. You do not become free. You realize you always were.

31. Love doesn't let you fall.

32. Love, don't let chu fall.

REACQUAINTED WITH LIFE

All I Have

I'mma melted cheese on my flamin hots eatin/playin tag while bullets flyin/iz time fo da perculata uh duh daz y we's perculatin perculatin/peppamint n penny candy n my pickle lip smackin/I can't tell time but so wat I'm still gon floss my gummi watch rockin/hey yaw dey finely got my overalls out da Goldblatt's layaway afta almos two years stuntin/da ice cream truck left bfo I cud tho my shoes on sobbin/Jezus is da answa fo da wurl today Calvary Missionary Baptist Church on na corna ah 87th n Stony Island cross da street from da KFC evry Sunday goin/dirty dirty dozens yo mama yo daddy yo greazy greazy granpappy playin/who you callin black bitch getcho big lookin azz u betta R.E.S.P.E.K. me demandin/ Uncle Remus ain't got shit on Harold's Chicken debatin/ bang bang bang skeet skeet skeet lemme see you juke jukin/ fuck you mean da Wesside betta at footwork defendin/los my virginity in ah abandoned garage I'll suck yo dick as long as you lumme u lumme don't you Rashan askin/use ta be boo boo da foo talkin bout he can do wateva he wants ta me so long as he got waves n lite skin thirstin/Rupaul waz my role model til I discovered Sylvester n Grace Jones evolvin/Moesha waz da gurl I swo I wud one day grow up ta b hopin/soufside Chi til u muthafuckin die reppin/hair ruffa denna Brillo pad/ skin darka denna Black N Mile/voice louda den a shootout tween da Moe's n na Foe's/wit sharpa den da blade ya boy use ta cut crack wit/yea dat b me/n whiles othaz may hide dey history/I plops like ah pig playin wit itz puzzy in mines/ cuz I know alls too well dat when na cam'ras stop rollin n awards stop bein received/I/will once again/be all I have.

Ursula's Lament

I'm not angry.
I'se anga!
Pregnant witta rage dat won't breach.
Crippled by wounds dat don't scab.
Perpetually in laba, n swimmin in my own damn blood.
Yop!
I do spit acid.
Sneeze carbon monoxide n shit black mambas too!
But see!
What I have?
Isn't a case of seeing the glass half-empty.
Or refusing to wake up, and smell the coffee.
I'm tryna tell yo ass da roas steamin outta yo cup?
Ain't da one simmrin in mines boo.
It's da receipt of my oppression.
Side-effect of havin tha body nobody wants.
N result
of bein born tha person
evrybody is tol ta never become.
Fat, black, n me.

When Escape Becomes Re-Entry

I dun run outta ways ta faget my pain.
Da methods I used seemed ta hurt me mo den u eva cud anyhow.
Waz doin yo dirty work n ain't eum knows it.
Ran so hard! Ain't eum notice my feets was busted n bleedin.
Ran so hard? Ain't eum notice, I neva stopped ta put on shoes!
Ain't dat sum shit?
Dun run cross dis wurl 3 times,
justa getta away from yo ass!
N hurt myself evry steppa ah da way.

Body Language

Pound!
Pound!
Pound!
Pound!
Pound!
He don't know words, he jus know sounds.
Tha soun of my saliva cascadin down da base of his dick.
Tha soun of my ass and his pelvic bone whisperin ta each otha.
Pound!
Pound!
Pound!
Pound!
Pound!
He don't know how ta say he lumme wit his mouf,
so he say it wittis fis'.
And I don't ask fa mo.
Cuz my vocabulary ain't that big eitha.

Black As Hell Blues

He said,
I need ah' red-bone witta fat ass.
Then commenced to lay me on his bed.
Hmph!
Story of my life
Always the conquerable exotic.
But never the bride.

Practice Makes Perfect

She said,
you practice on dark-skindid boys,
you marry, light-skint ones.
To hear, the tone.
The twisted, conviction.
The strategic delusion!
The axiom, that I should be grateful to be your victim.
The assumption, that my pain, is the psycho-social equivalent,
to a pair of training wheels.
This brand, of insanity leaves me with only two questions:
Why didn't anybody tell me I was just rehearsal?
And when did rape, become a fuckin' social service?

I Am The Child

I am the child
Who is the envy of evry ghetto "girl"
I am the child
Who was the intrigue of evry dough "boy"
I am the child
Whose body is played with
Like a freshly unwrapped Christmas toy

I'm Takin Back My Body

I'm takin back my body.
U dun played wit it, longgg, enuf.
Yeah I see ya hemmin n hawwin.
But I neva said yo ass cud have it in na firs place now did I?
You was weak.
I was convenient.
And nah hea we r.
You was lookin fa powa, and you found it, in, dis, hea, flesh.
I was yo science project, voodoo doll,
And playground all in fuckin one.
Yeah!
Ya hid ya secrets in me!
Even tricked me inta thinkin they was mines ta keep.
I can't go ten seconds witout yo lies searin thru my skin.
Hmph!
When did my body become yo ashtray?
N why am I jus now feelin da fuckin burn?
I'm takin back my body.
Gon dust it off,
take it to da cleanas,
open do's fa it,
hol it close when we watchin scary pictures,
sava tha kiss good night,
n spin aroun' like onna dem white bitches
In ah old powda face movie.
Happy!
Happy cuz sumbody dun gaves huh sumn beautiful.
You hea dat?
Fo da firs' time eva!
I'm gon gi myself sumn beautiful.
I'm gon gi myself?
Me!

I'se Gon Be Loved

One day imma be nestled!
Kissed in all my fav'rite places,
and called beautiful too.

A Diff'rent Kinda Eve

I don't wanna take yo place
I jus wanna know how it feel
how it feel ta know dat no matta how hard life is there
Will always be sumone waitin ta love you
how it feel ta not think sumbody holdin yo hand
in public
is an act of revolution
I wanna glow, have people think life growin inside ah me too
of course not like it grow inside you
but ah unique birf
I want you, n na whole wide wurl ta know I'se gettin gravid
say shit like, "yes I've neva been so happy in my life"
or, "I just can't seem ta decide on a name"
and my personal fav'rite, "heyyy yawl, I'm eatin fa two "
I neva wanted yo man, jus one brave enuf ta luv me
but dat's what I get fa thankin you was happy wit yern
but I'm not him, he beat you, not me
he left you ta raise dem kids, not me
you was so livid
you cudn't even realize dat I been dere
tha whole time
I was yo chile, I was the child, I am the child
So I taught myself
n got tha wounds n nightmares ta remind me
like I said gurl
I neva wanted ta take yo place
I jus wanted ta walk down da street in my sexy and not worry
I know da wurl dun did u wrong
I was right right dere when dey did it
but I'm not tha world, dey even tried ta force me to join in
and when you was drunk on yo pain you begged me ta too,
but I didn't

cuz I knewded sumn waz growin n me
no, not like dey grow in you, but how dey grows, in me
I know it sound funny n sum would e'um say m'postible
but I feels it,
a diff'rent kinda cycle,
a diff'rent kinda conception,
a diff'rent kinda trimester,
a diff'rent kinda pregnancy
See! See! See!
touch my stomach
Feel lat?
kickin, movin roun in my crawl,
thowin off my gravity
n bringin me back
I'se pregnant!
finna give birf!
to a diff'rent kinda goddess
not hea ta take anybody seat on the throne.
but ta take my rightful place amongst the pantheon

Class Dismissed

My body is not your thesis.
My body is not your learning curve.
My body is not your teachable moment.
My body is not your homework assignment.
My body is not the board
you hock broken erasors and spitballs at.
My body is not the desk you stick ABC gum under
or carve initials on.
My body is not the classroom.
My body is not the timid nerd you prod.
My body is not the weird kid you tease.
My body is not the popular asshole you fear.
My body, is the mysterious loner.
You know the archetype.
The one who gets the attention,
without ever trying to get it, or even wanting to have it.
The one who's not above fuckin a teacher for a better grade,
or shankin a bully ta even the score.
My body is that nasty bitch suckin off the security guards,
and cussin out the hatin ass hoes
who work in na principals office.
My body is the catboi breakin up
the busiest lunch period of the day,
just becuz I'se dun mastered the art,
of turning your torture, into my entertainment.
My body is tha firestarter
who will blow dis factory for fools sky high,
pile da bodies like Carrie at prom,
and eva so swiftly give you da finga,
all while lightin a blunt en route to da getaway car.
No doubt driven by da janita.
Oh yeahh!

I'm nasty like dat!
My body, is both your secret fantasy, and worst nightmare muthafuckas.
It's dark.
It's femme.
It's fat.
And it's gotdamn fuckin beautiful bitches.

Back To The Drawing Board

So you wanna revolution huh?
Aight I'm down!
Jus riddle me dis.
How it gon tase'?
Where we gon hide tha weapons?
Do we need em?
If so who got my bail money?
What gon be da new laws?
Is we gon ban da coloniza's language?
Can we go back ta worshippin r riginal god?
N will da folks dat don't wanna worship no gods at all be cool?
What's we's gon do bout da sexual offendas, freaks, n geeks?
N wat bout dem pesky ass white people?
Betta yet, wat about da light-skint peoples
Always playin bof sides da fence?
I cud go on longa than you cud listen shuga!
But what I really wanna know.
Is are you invested in making the world a better place for all?
Or just you and yours?

White Feminist Barbie

Aren't you tired of those clueless, submissive Barbies?
You know!
The ones that never check their privilege!
And are more concerned with their Malibu Dream Houses,
than liberating their Middle Eastern sisters from those
oppressive burqas?
Then meet White Feminist Barbie!
That's right!
White Feminist Barbie!
The latest creation from Mattel!
And she's not your mother's Barbie.
Uh uh!
She doesn't waste her days slaving away in the kitchen for
too busy Ken.
So meet Hakeem, White Feminist Barbie's boyfriend and weed man.
White Feminist Barbie, for the post-racial girl on the go.
White Feminist Barbie,
available at Toys R Us' across the nation this Kwanzaa.
White Feminist Barbie!

::Non-profit organization, distractingly ethnic fashion sense,
and delusional self-righteousness sold separately.

There Are No Exceptions

Whenever you sit down:
It's legs crossed.
Mouth shut.
Smile for the camera.
Wave to the hyenas.
Keep the exotic name.
But stand still while they banish that Africa from your hair.
Pout as they photo shop that disrespectful melanin.
Show them the aspect of your sexuality that enthralls them,
but bores you.
Do everything but practically rob, the federal reserve.
Turn one-hundred dollar bills into tampons.
Preach abstinence.
Get married.
And then, and only then.
Create life!
Child, it is indeed your destiny, to be a goddess.
But irregardless of how many records you break,
And spells you cast.
Whenever the world looks at you,
all it will ever see, is a whore.
And just when you were starting to believe you were special.
Right?

What About My Body

not anutha poem
not anutha movie
Zenobia corpse laid up in da French Quartas
like a runned ova possum
Milani head was ripped off huh body
like a ole track left out on Christopha Street
n I still, can't sleep on my back
where my national holiday?
where my creation story?
no tea!
no shade!
I get it,
evry 5 seconds a black binary woman is beaten
well evry 2.5 seconds, a "black"
non-binary femme or person is beaten,
then killed.
I'm done advocatin
I'm through, empathizin
she ain't no mo tiyad ah gettin huh ass whooped den me
not anutha pamphlet
not anutha intervention
fuck tha dumb shit!
quiet as it's kept evry time I've eva been raped,
there was a binary black woman eitha eggin na shit on,
or joinin in onna got-dam fun
why don't my screams warrant da police?
why don't my psychosis warrant a savior?
I wanna fuckin know!
I wanna, fuckin, know!
I said I wanna fuckin know!
What about my body?

A Hug I Can Live In

Mos people go thu life doin alla things on purpose
I cudn't do by accident.
I see em evryday.
Jus spillin inta life.
Knowin it don't matta how close dey get to dat cliff,
iz always gon be sumbody dea ready ta bring em back.
Bring m back ta love, ta land, ta home.
And do it witta hug!
A hug they can live in.
Yeah, buddy!
Dog pissin n tornadoes n squirtin wata guns at thundabolts.
You see em!
Hittin da Lucky Lotto
wen dey ass ain't even bought a cot-damn ticket.
While me on da otha hand?
All I knows is turned backs, n broken promises.
Buildin a life outta alla things otha people dun thu away.
N bein first in na line ta nowhea.
But evry now n again,
You know,
afta I've found a place safe enuf ta not be murdered in?
I wunda.
Will I eva find a hug?
One I can I live in?

Love Is Not The Revolution

Who gon hol me?
Hol me when da flashbacks start n I can't be comforted.
But I want you ta try anyway.
I needs, you ta try, anyway!
I'm tiyad ah speakin ah truf don't nobody wanna hea.
I'm tiyad ah fightin fa otha people's right ta have a love
I ain't gon eva kno.
Been shoutin from mountain tops longa den Moses n Martin.
Fightin from trenches longa than ya fav'rite fuckin war hero.
But who gon help me down dough?
Who gon unclench my fist n tho da grenades placed n my hand?
Not cuz I eva wanted em.
But cuz ain't nobody else hah my aim!
You see, contrary ta popula belief.
Samurai don't really relish solitude,
They simply master the art of living alone.
And sometimes, even tornadoes are embarrassed,
By the devastation they wield.
All, I wants, iz sumbody ta lumme.
I dun bent realities, toppled regimes,
and freed slaves Harriet Tub style!
But, who, gon, luh, me?
Lumme when I puts down, da bullhorn?
Massage my feets afta, da tenf mile ah da thirty-six march?
N I ain't da mos poppin activis on da block no mo?
I'se dun released enuf hot air ta extinguish da sun.
N cried enuf tears ta supply ah wata park big enuf,
Fa evry orphan in Haiti.
Nah who gon lumme?
Not becuz I'm weak!
But becuz I'm tiyad ah havin ta be so goddamn invincible.

The Poem My Desperation Wrote

I'll give you me in evry way I come.
Entertain you, overlook your flaws,
and even ignore my better judgment.
Ain't no grudge, worth my happiness right?
Without you even havin ta ask,
I'll show you tha softa side ah me.
Hell, might eum go numb!
All I ask, is that you treat me like a lady.
Faget tha fact that most people will neva,
see me as a woman,
and I have no memories of eva, truly, being a girl.
Nonetheless!
Lay with me.
Yes, I will be pitiful.
But you will be satisfied.

I Pray For A Love

I pray for a love.
One that picks me up.
Not ask why am I on the ground.
I pray for a love.
One that doesn't see my flaws, as deal-breakers
while its, are selling points.
I pray for a love.
One I ain't gotta perform, or, audition fo'.
I pray for a love.
One that's mine.
All mine.
So I can be its.
All, its.
I pray for a love.
That'll soothe alla storms helling, underneath my skin.
Turning my salt water?
Into tonic!
I pray for a love.
And it's like
waitin onna package from sumbody
dat ain't eum got cho address.
Or waitin' onna day ah da week, dat ain't neva gon' come.
Yet and still.
I'se pray for a love.
But more than anything.
I pray fa arms, strong enuf' ta holds it.

I Came To Jesus (He Came In My Hair)

I came to Jesus
naked as the day I was born
after being born again, on a hospital bed
I showed him the body he gave me
but I made vast improvements upon
and since beauty is in the eyes of the beholder
before we parted, I made sure ta give em a lap dance
so he cud see dat ass bounce up n down!

First Things First

U thank this da firs' time I been raped?
Hurry up: Moesha finna come on!
U thank this da firs' time I been raped?
Hurry up: My bus come in fideen minutes!
U thank this da firs' time I been raped?
Hurry up: My mama comin home from work soon!
U thank this da firs' time I been raped?
Hurry up: My popcorn burnin!
U thank this da firs' time I been raped?
Hurry up: How long dis gon take, I'll call Uber!
U thank this da firs' time I been raped?
Hurry up: What no foreplay?
U thank this da firs' time I been raped?
Hurry up: Ya wife look like she wanna turn!
U thank this da firs' time I been raped?
Hurry up: Ya dog too!
U thank this da firs' time I been raped?
Hurry up: No video-recordin, or flash photography!
U thank this da firs' time I been raped?
Hurry up: One at a time!
U thank this da firs' time I been raped?
Hurry up: Next time, don't wake me!

Bedtime Stories

Tanite I'm sleepin on my back.
N ain't nobody gon jimmy open da do'.
Or even knock it down drunk.
Tanite, I'mma touch myself.
N fa once, not have flashbacks.
Huh mouf, his hands, they lafta.
Tanite, I'mma sleep on my back.
Not piss on myself ta ward off the unwelcomed visitas.
Not cement myself on my gut as a las ditch effort.
I'mma rest tonight.
I'mma dream.
Dream dat dream I was dreamin da first time I eva woke up ta.
Huh, him, n dem.
Havin ney way,
n showin me God's.

Cycle Of Self-Inflicted Abuse
(Lifetime 'Til Happy)

scream n hand
cry at reflection
faget dat I'm ugly
keep dancin
eat beyond fill
drink enuf ta flush out yestaday
tuck my dick
put munny n my puzzy ja'
sit on toilet
ask why they thought they cud touch me like dat
yell at child posin as my stomach
ta make way fo da six-pack en-route
look out window
wish my pillow wud marry me
watch tv
imagine myself as sumbody not pathetic,
revel at how much easier life wud be
if I was skinny, lite-skint, n a "real woman"
masturbate
repeat compliments I don't believe
pray off suicide
pace
survive
hurt
create
binge
dream
repeat

Psych Ward Soliloquy

Bipolar!
Anti-social!
Egomaniacal!
Schizophrenic!
Megalomaniacal!
Yaw'll calla black bitch anything but right.

Justice (This Is The Remix)

Lemmetellusumn!
Bein a victim,
ain't nearly as sexy,
as they make it look in nem Lifetime movies.
I mean when you ain't, actually, Brooke Shields?
You don't get nice nurses,
lilac n chrysanthemum arrangements,
orra room witta view.
When folk like me is beaten n raped,
or fortunate enuf ta get da 2 fa 1 special.
Da chieffa police won't give you time, ta, cry,
let alone a fuckin cuppa cwoffee.
When folk like me in dis hea wonderful world is attacked.
We don't get justice.
We get wisa'

Apology Panderin'

I don't need to learn how to forgive anybody.
You, need to learn how to stop hurting people.

Survivor's Guide

I am not what you did to me.
I am not what you did to me.
I am not what you did to me.
I am not what you did to me.
I am not what you did to me.
I am not what you did to me.
I am not what you did to me.
I am not what you did to me.
I am not what you did to me.
I am not what you did to me.
I am not what you did to me.

When The Mirror Spoke Back (Hey Jada)

They'll give you money,
before they ever give you
freedom.

Vampire In Brooklyn, Chicago, Hollywood Et Al

Vampires are real.
As a matta ah fack, ya sittin cross from em rite nah in Popeye's.
Or dat high-class joint dey like goin ta evry Sataday nite,
afta a weeka soul, suckin.
Toastin!
Swingin dey head back!
N smilin like pretense finna go outta style.
Laughin at otha people expense but, swearin dey saved.
Girlll, vampires is real, azza muhfucka.
In the White House.
On the red carpet.
Da corna office.
N headed to da walk a fame.
Dey dun founna way ta hide they fangs.
But if you putta mirra ta dat ass,
neitha one ah yaw wud see a reflection.
I'm tryna tell u chile, vampires is realll!
Standin behind pulpits.
Even holdin na picket sign.
They slap on na sunblock and keep it muthafuckin, movin.
Suckin yo life force witta a false smile,
fake-ass lease on life,and a cute hashtag.
They trick u inta thankin dey actually give two shits about ya.
Girl boom!
Don't be fooled.
Vampires are real.
N ney don't show love.
They show patronage!
Why?
Becuzzz!
You ain't shit ta dem, but a bank, bench,
or muthafuckin bodega.

The hatstand they hang their dreams on.
N na las pieca bacon dey bite bfo dey do a fuckin,
Atkin's cleanse.
So uuu, jus rememba!
All mythological creatures don't exist unda bridges or
sleep n coffins.
Summa dem bitchez is "buildin" witcha rite nah, or
hoggin da covas.
Cuz contrary ta popula belief,
vampires don't need blood.
Just your energy.

Psychological Share-Croppin'

Get tha fuck off me, muthafuckas!
The constant triangulation!
The convenient respectability!
Then ta top it allll off.
Presto-chango-alakazaam!
My pain, is now magically your platform.
I ask you.
When did community become a form of currency?
They only love you as long as they can use you.
They only show up when the bodies hit the ground.
And eum then, it's just ta take pictures ova da corpse.
Shh!
Shh!
Shh!
U hea dat?
Iz da soun ah my bonez
whistlin from u suckin em dry fa sound bites.
Iz da soun of my joints poppin from overextendin
demselves fa people who'd neva return da fava!
They made it illegal ta hunt elephants.
But wat dey shudda outlawed, was u unoriginal,
pedestrian ass muthafuckas,
from bitin da analysis of actual intellects,
via da social media milieu.
The devil, is in the DM's and subtweets my nigga.
The DM's, and subtweets, my nigga!
Niggaz swea upndown, dey been sent from da burnin bush.
When alley did waz bite yo analysis,
n slap da face odda right typa wrong on it.
But you should be so lucky,
if any of the assorted market-made messiahs,
do decide ta, "amplify" your voice.

Jus don't be surprised if dat amplification
look mo like da muzzlin offa rabid dog.
Cuz make no mistakes about it,
datz precisely what you are ta dem.
A dog.
A dog barkin n bitin at da heels ah da good nice white folks.
N we's can't have de undesirables,
fuckin it up fa da beautiful people.
Now can we?
They eat first ugly.
And if you're good!
You get to lick their fingers.
Imma jus say it like dis.
As long as progress is gauged by strides in assimilation,
we're all doomed.

Erasure Is Rape In Reverse

Erasure is rape in reverse.
Because with rape.
They take your body, then silence your voice.
But with erasure.
They take your voice, then silence your body.

The Fame Monster (To The POC/LGBT Elite) (Part Une)

You all?
Are nothing more,
than the ring leaders of a circus for abominations.
With the nerve ta b choicey,
bout who get ta hop through the hoops.

Making Money Is Not Shining

Making money is not shining.
The sun lights an entire solar system.
And hasn't a penny to its name.

The Fame Monster (To The POC/LGBT Elite) (Part Deux)

There is nothing wrong with wanting to be famous.
There is something wrong,
with writing your autograph in other people's blood.

Dear John Letter To The Movement

I do have a mental problem.
And it's called you.
Good bye!

The Last Apology

And they were loud.
Chile, dey, was, loud!
Ate wings n drank wine!
High-fived n finga-snapped!
Talk shit n testified!
Summoned da ancestas n eum created room
at da grown folk table fada chillins.
Girl, do ya's hea me when I tell ya?
I say, dey was loud!
Loud, trans, queer, n black.
N fada firs' time eva.
Dey wadn't nowhea nea sorry bouts it.

Reacquainted With Life

wade through rocks
punch fist through earth
reach for the moon as if it were a life preserver
climb out one limb at a time
spit out worms
gnaw mold from fingertips
wipe eyes of tears and dirt
massage throat
allow fatigue
clinch torso
awaken voice
then find pride in where I lay
wounded, but alive

A Girl Can Dream

tongue kiss evry stretch mark
walk out inna summatime hopin I get darka
don't shave fa two monts n wave ta strangas like Princess Di
allow the wind ta pick up my dress n
give a wink ta whosoeva finds Waldo
drop my voice four octaves
and at dat moment feel my daintiest
introduce myself as my birth name
and wish a muthafucka wud call me sir
one day,
imma wake up in da monin
look dat mirra square in da face
and finally find beauty in all tha things I ain't suppose to

Beauty Is My Revenge

each wig represents a world/one I hope to become a part of/in my line of work femininity exists in a land of fantasy/ where songs rival the impact of bombs and dresses are loaded with more artillery than tanks/excuse me if I sound unrealistic/but the world has entitled me to only my dreams/ unfortunately the necessity of survival always trumps the longing for escape/reality witnesses me saving tips to a place where my body is more than just your entertainment/one day imma dance to original material/fling back my head and listen to folks reciting my lyrics with abandon/choreographin productions ta my virtuosity/bendin hardwood floors/splittin vocal chords to the soundtrack of my evolution/in my story imma princess/I use garters, satin, duct tape, and oil sheen as my weapons of choice/I go into battle not with a metal suit/but girdled silhouette/those who take me as jest come to dey senses when the spotlight touches me/equipped wif countless facial contortions and arm gesticulations/I undo the memory of your favorite antiquated idol/ocean of hair/ mountain of body/I can be reached through only a punctual high-five, organic work bitch, or demurely folded dollar bill/gather around children and let me tell you the story of one who from the bottom of nowhere/built dazzling spectacle from nothing more than wardrobe, imagination, and insanity/once upon a time/there was a queen, no, a goddess, with a penis/and she lived, happily, ever, after!

Kiam Marcelo Jr.

About The Author

She eats planets like jawbreakers.
Keeps dinosaurs as pets.
Turns asteroids into sex toys.
And her wardrobe consists of cosmic entities,
Fashioned into garments.
Water was created after she squirted,
Whilst being dog-fucked by her ex, God.
And fire, was crafted just ta light huh blunts.
When she snaps her fingers, universes appear.
When she smacks her lips, they vanish.
She created your sun, just, to dry her manicure.
And keeps the vacuum of space gusty
All so her makeup won't smudge.
Every deity, eva' worshipped.
Is but a hearty imitation.
And every religion, eva' established.
Is but a pathetic attempt at recreating the way
We once worshipped her as stars.
Yet she answers not to a name, only a frequency.
Attune and behold
KOKUMỌ!
The Original Goddess...

Fᴜᴄᴋ U's

*(In lieu of Thank You's, considerin how they luh callin me such ah
ungrateful bitch n all)*

Ta evry light-skinned person who thought I was ova-exaggeratin.
Fuck you bitch!
Ta evry dark-skinned person who thought we'd look odd tagetha.
Fuck you bitch!
Ta evry person who raped me like it was sum typa social service.
Fuck you bitch!
Ta evry white person who tol me ta tell my story,
but leave out that whole racism part.
Fuck you bitch!
Ta evry non-black POC who rides my pain
like the lone ranger on nat cot-damn horse.
Fuck you bitch!
Ta evry advocate
who only advocates for those who meet your criteria,
n activist who only acts when it's in their, best interest.
Fuck you bitch!
Ta evry feminist n womanist
who treats/treated me like the actual man who raped them,
all the while slappin my ass n gropin my titties
cuz dey can't believe it's not butta.
Fuck you bitch!

Ta evry elda who thinks wisdom comes from
age and not experience,
but can't explain why there are so many old fools.
Fuck you bitch!
Ta evry person in the Trans Movement who deemed me good
enuf to siphon from, mock, n good ole-fashion mammify,
but not worship, love, and properly compensate.
Fuck you bitch!
Ta evry pseudo-intellectual, quasi-revolutionary, fake-deep ass
muhfucka who thank a po', dark-skint intersex, gnc, fat
femme sayin bitch, is misogynistic cuz they clearly have
no sense ah privilege matriculation, n ney systems analysis
might as well came outta crack jack box.
Fuck, you bitch!
N ta anybody, who will eva, even contemplate,
attempting to oppress me.
Fuck you? In advance.
Enjoy my book!

Acknowledgement

To all I've hurt:
Sometimes the gift, is pain.

To all who've hurt me:
Your betrayal, was my baptism.

Ase...

KOKUMỌ

About Heliotrope

Heliotrope is a dedicated series of poetry books by transgender authors. We value writing which which tells a story (or several) and is not only beautiful, but useful to its audiences.

In 2016, Heliotrope will publish books by KOKUMO, Cat Fitzpatrick and Kay Ulanday Barrett.

Heliotrope is an imprint of Topside Press and is edited by Cat Fitzpatrick. Cat teaches literature at Rutgers University - Newark and organizes the Trans Poets Workshop NYC.

Poets are welcome to join the Trans Poets Workshop- more information at transpoets.com

Submissions of poetry manuscripts are welcome year-round to cat@topsidepress.com

63371318R00037

Made in the USA
Charleston, SC
31 October 2016